MW00444764

California
Workbook

7th grade and 8th grade

120 Printable Activities

C. Mahoney

Life is about choices…

California Missions

What do you notice about these two stamps?

John Muir

What do you notice about this coin and stamp honoring John Muir?

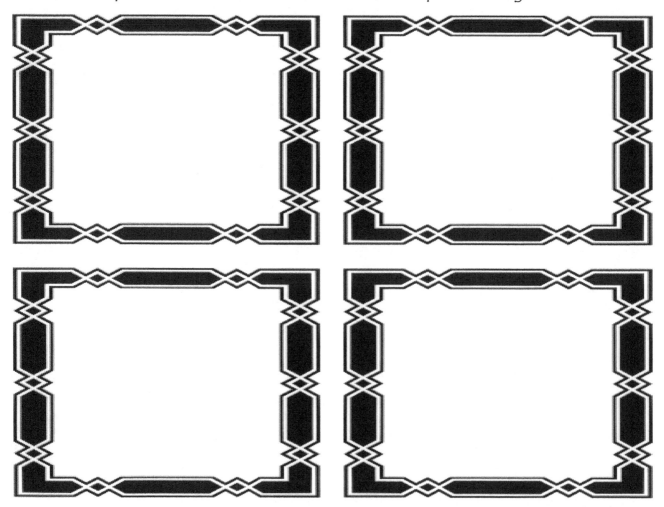

Business

Analyze this stamp and write down the interesting things you notice about its <u>words</u>, <u>numbers</u> and <u>pictures</u>.

Hollywood Films

What do you notice about these stamps?

California Politics

What do you notice about these stamps honoring Ronald Reagan?

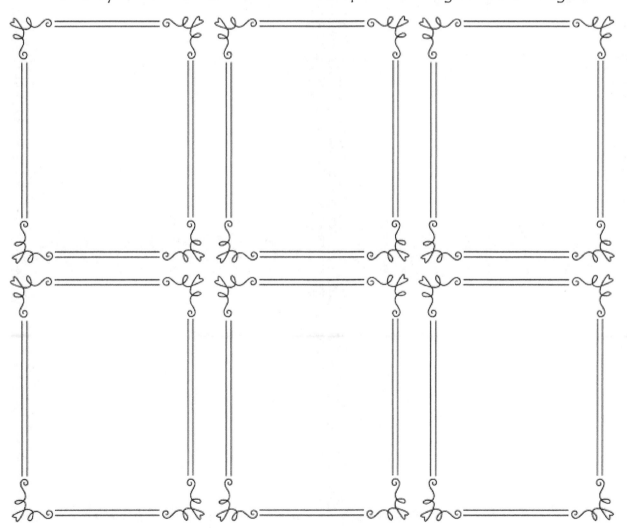

California Movies

What do you notice about these stamps honoring Disney movies?

Explaining Why...

Which one of these four stamps is the **best**? _____

Explain **why**: _____

_____

_____

_____

_____

_____

Explaining Why...

Which one of these four stamps is the **<u>best</u>**? _____

Explain **<u>why</u>**: _____

_____

_____

_____

_____

_____

Describing California Symbols #7

Directions: <u>Describe</u> FIVE things that you notice about each **California** image.

scales
1
2
3
4
5

a ticket
1
2
3
4
5

movie reels
1
2
3
4
5

bikes
1
2
3
4
5

Describing California Symbols #8

Directions: <u>Describe</u> FIVE things that you notice about each **California** image.

a speed limit sign

1
2
3
4
5

the Naughty or Nice list

1
2
3
4
5

a father

1
2
3
4
5

a baseball player

1
2
3
4
5

Describing California Symbols #9

Directions: <u>Describe</u> FIVE things that you notice about each **California** image.

the beach

1
2
3
4
5

a boombox

1
2
3
4
5

restaurant signs

1
2
3
4
5

a basketball

1
2
3
4
5

Describing California Symbols #10

Directions: <u>Describe</u> FIVE things that you notice about each **California** image.

a kite

1
2
3
4
5

the California outline

1
2
3
4
5

a dog

1
2
3
4
5

a surfer

1
2
3
4
5

Comparing Movement

Describe the things you notice about these activities.

things that move   **things that do not move**

1.   1.

2.   2.

3.   3.

4.   4.

5.   5.

Comparing Emotions

Describe the things you notice about these emotions.

on the inside (where people cannot see)	**on the outside** (where people can see)
1.	1.
2.	2.
3.	3.
4.	4.
5.	5.

Comparing Mental States

wide-awake   **asleep**

Write four things you notice about these two different states.

1 _____
_____
_____
_____

2 _____
_____
_____

3 _____
_____
_____

4 _____
_____
_____

Comparing Body Parts

Think about how a <u>person</u> and <u>dog</u> use their body to move in this activity: who is pulling (or being pulled), who decides where to go, who makes the most noise, who gets to decide...

Hands

1

Feet

2

Body

3

Comparing Vehicles

Analyze these two moving vehicles. How do they move? Who rides inside? What do they carry? What are they made of? What is their purpose? Are either real or fake? When do we see them?

1 _____
_____
_____

2 _____
_____
_____

3 _____
_____

4 _____
_____

5 _____
_____

Comparing Friends

How are animals similar to people?

1 _____
_____
_____

2 _____
_____
_____

3 _____
_____
_____

4 _____
_____
_____

Comparing Youngsters

**an emotional
young monkey**

**a calm
young human**

Think about <u>when</u> they play, and <u>where</u>, and <u>why</u>, and by themselves or with a friend, and during the daytime or at night, and who watches over them…

Comparing Foods

natural food

processed food

List FOUR things that you notice about these types of meals:

1 _____
_____
_____

2 _____
_____
_____

3 _____
_____
_____

4 _____
_____
_____

Comparing Dragons

List FIVE things that you know about these two flying critters.

1 _____
_____
_____

2 _____
_____
_____

3 _____
_____
_____

4 _____
_____
_____

5 _____
_____
_____

Grover Hot Springs State Park

Search for interesting facts about this California tourist destination. What are its most interesting features? Why do people travel there and explore? What is so amazing about this place?

ONLINE SOURCES OF INFORMATION:

California's Forests

Search online for interesting facts about California's forests. Discover something odd or amazing about its trees or the animals that live there.

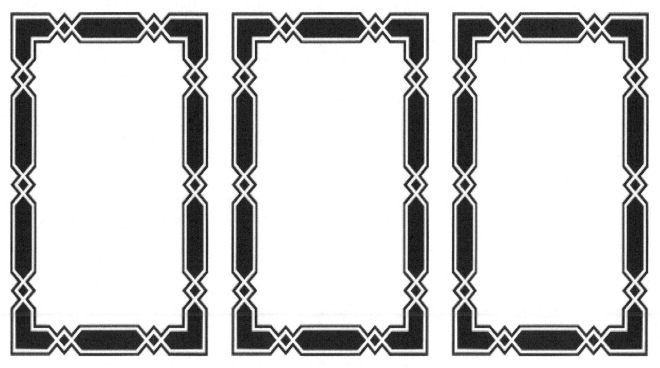

ONLINE SOURCES OF INFORMATION:

_____

_____

California's Coasts

Search online for interesting facts about California's beaches. Discover something odd or amazing about the coast and how the water affects the land and animals at its edges.

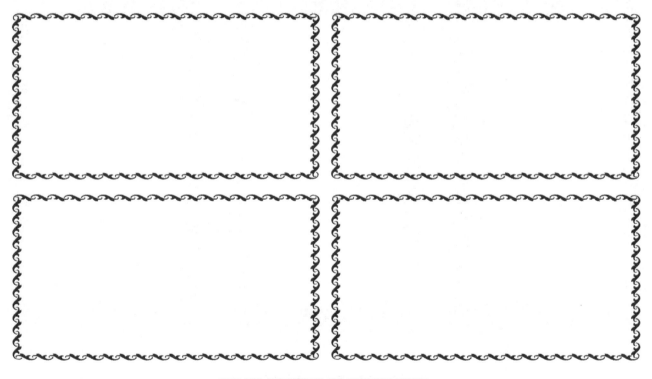

ONLINE SOURCES OF INFORMATION:

_____

_____

California's Deserts

Search online for interesting facts about California's deserts. Discover something odd or amazing about the plants or the animals that call this place "home".

1

2

3

4

ONLINE SOURCES OF INFORMATION:

_____

_____

California's Plains

Search online for interesting facts about California's plains. Discover something odd or amazing about its grass and flowers and the animals that survive there year-round.

ONLINE SOURCES OF INFORMATION:

California's Mountains

Search online for interesting facts about California's mountains. Discover something odd or amazing about its weather and shape and how they got to be there.

1

2

3

4

ONLINE SOURCES OF INFORMATION: :

_____

_____

California

What is so amazing about the state of California?

1.

2.

3.

4.

5.

6.

7.

8.

9.

10.

ONLINE SOURCES OF INFORMATION:

_____

_____

Exploring the Outdoors in California

List ten activities that you can do wearing hiking boots in California:

1.

2.

3.

4.

5.

6.

7.

8.

9.

10.

ONLINE SOURCES OF INFORMATION:

_____

_____

CALIFORNIA TRAILS

What are the benefits of exploring the outdoors in California?

1.

2.

3.

4.

5.

6.

7.

8.

9.

10.

ONLINE SOURCES OF INFORMATION:

_____

_____

California State Parks

Search online for interesting facts about California's State Parks.

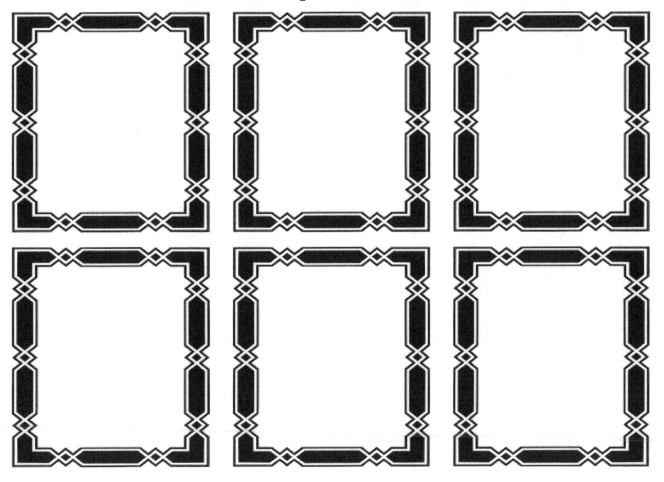

ONLINE SOURCES OF INFORMATION:

_____

_____

Decoding California Symbols *#16*

Analyze each California image and decode its secrets. What do the letters and images represent? They are there for a reason. Figure it out and write what you notice.

What <u>letters</u> or <u>words</u> do you see?

What <u>things</u> or <u>objects</u> do you see?

What **business** or **organization** is this symbol for?

What <u>letters</u> or <u>words</u> do you see?

What <u>things</u> or <u>objects</u> do you see?

What **business** or **organization** is this symbol for?

What <u>letters</u> or <u>words</u> do you see?

What <u>things</u> or <u>objects</u> do you see?

What **business** or **organization** is this symbol for?

Decoding California Symbols #17

Analyze each California image and decode its secrets. What do the letters and images represent? They are there for a reason. Figure it out and write what you notice.

What <u>letters</u> or <u>words</u> do you see?	What <u>letters</u> or <u>words</u> do you see?	What <u>letters</u> or <u>words</u> do you see?
What <u>things</u> or <u>objects</u> do you see?	What <u>things</u> or <u>objects</u> do you see?	What <u>things</u> or <u>objects</u> do you see?
What **business** or **organization** is this symbol for?	What **business** or **organization** is this symbol for?	What **business** or **organization** is this symbol for?

Decoding California Symbols #18

Analyze each California image and decode its secrets. What do the letters and images represent? They are there for a reason. Figure it out and write what you notice.

What <u>letters</u> or <u>words</u> do you see?

What <u>things</u> or <u>objects</u> do you see?

What **business** or **organization** is this symbol for?

What <u>letters</u> or <u>words</u> do you see?

What <u>things</u> or <u>objects</u> do you see?

What **business** or **organization** is this symbol for?

What <u>letters</u> or <u>words</u> do you see?

What <u>things</u> or <u>objects</u> do you see?

What **business** or **organization** is this symbol for?

Decoding California Symbols #19

Analyze each California image and decode its secrets. What do the letters and images represent? They are there for a reason. Figure it out and write what you notice.

What <u>letters</u> or <u>words</u> do you see?	What <u>letters</u> or <u>words</u> do you see?	What <u>letters</u> or <u>words</u> do you see?
What <u>things</u> or <u>objects</u> do you see?	What <u>things</u> or <u>objects</u> do you see?	What <u>things</u> or <u>objects</u> do you see?
What **business** or **organization** is this symbol for?	What **business** or **organization** is this symbol for?	What **business** or **organization** is this symbol for?

Decoding California Symbols #20

Analyze each California image and decode its secrets. What do the letters and images represent? They are there for a reason. Figure it out and write what you notice.

What <u>letters</u> or <u>words</u> do you see?

What <u>things</u> or <u>objects</u> do you see?

What **business** or **organization** is this symbol for?

What <u>letters</u> or <u>words</u> do you see?

What <u>things</u> or <u>objects</u> do you see?

What **business** or **organization** is this symbol for?

What <u>letters</u> or <u>words</u> do you see?

What <u>things</u> or <u>objects</u> do you see?

What **business** or **organization** is this symbol for?

Decoding California Symbols *#21*

Analyze each California image and decode its secrets. What do the letters and images represent? They are there for a reason. Figure it out and write what you notice.

What <u>letters</u> or <u>words</u> do you see?	What <u>letters</u> or <u>words</u> do you see?	What <u>letters</u> or <u>words</u> do you see?
What <u>things</u> or <u>objects</u> do you see?	What <u>things</u> or <u>objects</u> do you see?	What <u>things</u> or <u>objects</u> do you see?
What **business** or **organization** is this symbol for?	What **business** or **organization** is this symbol for?	What **business** or **organization** is this symbol for?

California Dogface Butterfly
California State Insect

Use a <u>laptop</u>, <u>tablet</u> or <u>phone</u> to access the internet and explore this **insect**. Record several interesting facts you discovered in your research.

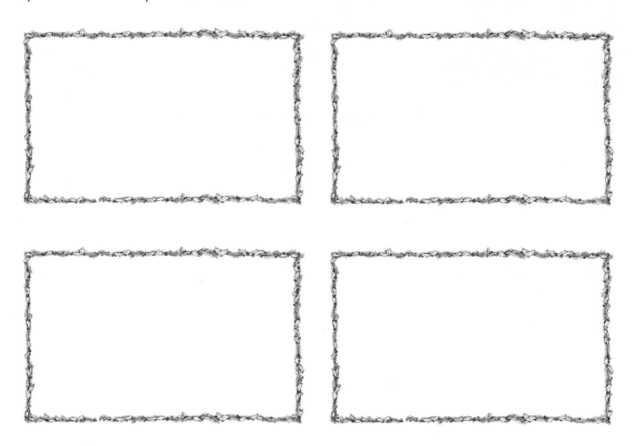

SOURCES:

_____

_____

Garibaldi

California State Marine Fish

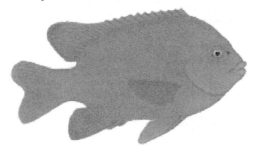

Use a <u>laptop</u>, <u>tablet</u> or <u>phone</u> to access the internet and explore this **marine fish**. Record several interesting facts you discovered in your research.

1 _____
_____
_____

2 _____
_____
_____

3 _____
_____
_____

4 _____
_____
_____

5 _____
_____
_____

SOURCES:

_____

_____

Gray Whale
California State Marine Mammal

Use a <u>laptop</u>, <u>tablet</u> or <u>phone</u> to access the internet and explore this **marine mammal**. Record several interesting facts you discovered in your research.

1
_____
_____
_____

2
_____
_____
_____

3
_____
_____
_____

4
_____
_____
_____

5
_____
_____
_____

SOURCES:

_____
_____

California Quarter

California State Quarter

Use a <u>laptop</u>, <u>tablet</u> or <u>phone</u> to access the internet and explore this **coin**. Record several interesting facts you discovered in your research about why these images and words are on the quarter.

1

2

3

4

SOURCES:

Eureka!

California State Motto

Use a <u>laptop</u>, <u>tablet</u> or <u>phone</u> to access the internet and explore this **motto**. Record several interesting facts you discovered in your research about this word and who said it in history.

SOURCES:

Serpentine

California State Rock

Use a <u>laptop</u>, <u>tablet</u> or <u>phone</u> to access the internet and explore this **rock**. Record several interesting facts you discovered in your research.

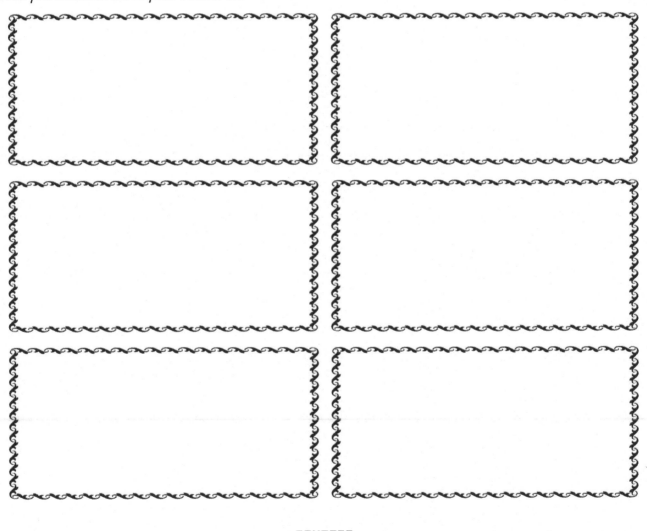

SOURCES:

_____

_____

"I Love You, California"

California State Song

Use a <u>laptop</u>, <u>tablet</u> or <u>phone</u> to access the internet and explore this **song**. Record several interesting facts you discovered in your research about the lyrics and why this song is important.

_____

_____

_____

_____

_____

_____

_____

_____

_____

_____

_____

_____

_____

_____

_____

_____

_____

_____

SOURCES:

_____

_____

Chipped Stone Bear
California State Artifact

Use a <u>laptop</u>, <u>tablet</u> or <u>phone</u> to access the internet and explore this **ancient artifact**. Record several interesting facts you discovered in your research.

SOURCES:

California Redwood

California State Tree

Use a <u>laptop</u>, <u>tablet</u> or <u>phone</u> to access the internet and explore this **tree**. Record several interesting facts you discovered in your research.

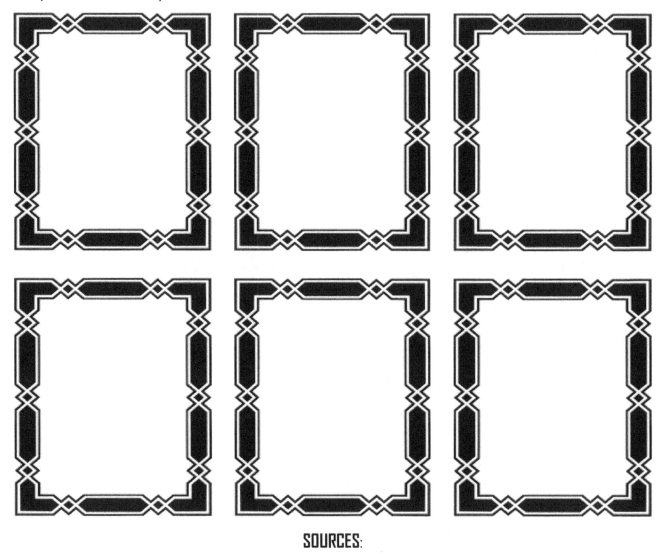

SOURCES:

_____

_____

La Purisma Mission

Use a laptop, tablet or phone to access the internet and explore this history of this mission.

Who founded it?

What is special about its name?

When was it founded?

Where is it located?

Search for four interesting facts about this mission and write them below:

SOURCES:

_____

_____

Mission San Francisco Solano

Use a laptop, tablet or phone to access the internet and explore this history of this mission.

Who founded it?

What is special about its name?

When was it founded?

Where is it located?

Search for four interesting facts about this mission and write them below:

SOURCES:

Mission San Buenaventura

Use a laptop, tablet or phone to access the internet and explore this history of this mission.

Who founded it?

What is special about its name?

When was it founded?

Where is it located?

Search for several interesting facts about this mission and write them below:

SOURCES:

_____

_____

Mission San Gabriel Arcángel

Use a laptop, tablet or phone to access the internet and explore this history of this mission.

Who founded it?

What is special about its name?

When was it founded?

Where is it located?

Search for three interesting facts about this mission and write them below:

1. _____
   _____
   _____
   SOURCE: _____

2. _____
   _____
   _____
   SOURCE: _____

3. _____
   _____
   _____
   SOURCE: _____

Mission San Luis Rey Francia

Use a laptop, tablet or phone to access the internet and explore this history of this mission.

Who founded it?

What is special about its name?

When was it founded?

Where is it located?

Search for four interesting facts about this mission and write them below:

SOURCES:

Mission Santa Inés

Use a laptop, tablet or phone to access the internet and explore this history of this mission.

<u>Who</u> founded it?

<u>What</u> is special about its name?

<u>When</u> was it founded?

<u>Where</u> is it located?

Search for four interesting facts about this mission and write them below:

 1

 2

 3

 4

SOURCES:

_____

_____

Mission San Carlos Borroméo del río Carmelo

Use a laptop, tablet or phone to access the internet and explore this history of this mission.

Who founded it?

What is special about its name?

When was it founded?

Where is it located?

Search for two interesting facts about this mission and write them below:

SOURCES:

California Missions

Use a laptop, tablet or phone to access the internet and explore the California Missions. Write ten interesting facts you discovered about them.

1.

2.

3.

4.

5.

6.

7.

8.

9.

10.

SOURCES:

_____

_____

Father Serra

Use a <u>laptop,</u> <u>tablet</u> or <u>phone</u> to access the internet and explore the life of Junipero Serra.
Write ten interesting facts you discovered about him.

1.

2.

3.

4.

5.

6.

7.

8.

9.

10.

SOURCES:

_____

_____

Evaluating What Californian's Say

Jim Morrison

singer and songwriter, director and actor

1	2	3
"A friend is someone who gives you total freedom to be yourself."	"Expose yourself to your deepest fear; after that, fear has no power, and the fear of freedom shrinks and vanishes."	"There are things known and things unknown and in between are the doors."

What do you fear?

_____

_____

_____

_____

What are four qualities of being a good friend that you have shown to others?

Evaluating What Californian's Say

Russell Westbrook
professional basketball player from Long Beach

1

"I always had to prove myself to people growing up. I had to show them that I could do this and I could do that, and paying no mind to what the critics said."

2

"Every day when I get on the floor I give it my all and play, because you never know what tomorrow holds."

3

"I say 'Why not?' to everything."

Have people told you that you can't do something, but you know you can?

_____

_____

_____

_____

_____

When did you give it your all, in sports or in a project, at home or in school?

_____

_____

_____

_____

Evaluating What Californian's Say

Tiger Woods

professional golfer from Cypress, California

1

"If you are given a chance to be a role model, I think you should always take it, because you can influence a person's life."

2

"People don't understand that when I grew up, I was never the most talented. I was never the biggest, I was never the fastest. I certainly was never the strongest. The only thing I had was my work ethic, and that's been what has gotten me this far."

3

"As I kid, I used to throw golf balls in the trees and try and somehow make par from them. I thought it was fun."

How can a professional athlete be a role model?

_____

_____

_____

_____

_____

Are you a super-achiever?

☐ – YES

☐ – NO

Explain:

Evaluating What Californian's Say

Sally Ride

Physicist and NASA astronaut from La Jolla, California

1

"All adventures, especially into new territories, are scary."

2

"Rocket science is hard, and rockets have a way of failing."

3

"My parents must have done a great job. Anytime I wanted to pursue something that they weren't familiar with, that was not part of their lifestyle, they let me go ahead and do it."

Think about your parents and how they encourage you to try new challenges:

...easy challenges

...tough challenges

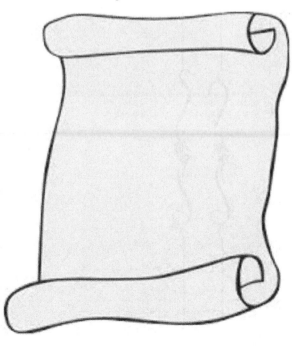

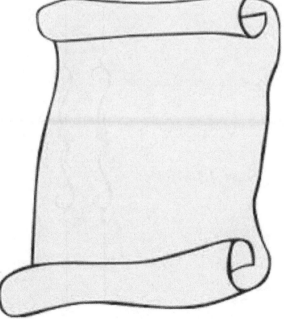

Evaluating What Californian's Say

Bruce Lee

martial artist, actor, director, screen writer from San Francisco

1

"Knowledge will give you power, but character respect."

2

"Mistakes are always forgivable, if one has the courage to admit them."

3

"If you love life, don't waste time, for time is what life is made of."

Share your thoughts on these key words spoken by Bruce Lee:

"character"　　　　　　"mistakes"　　　　　　"time"

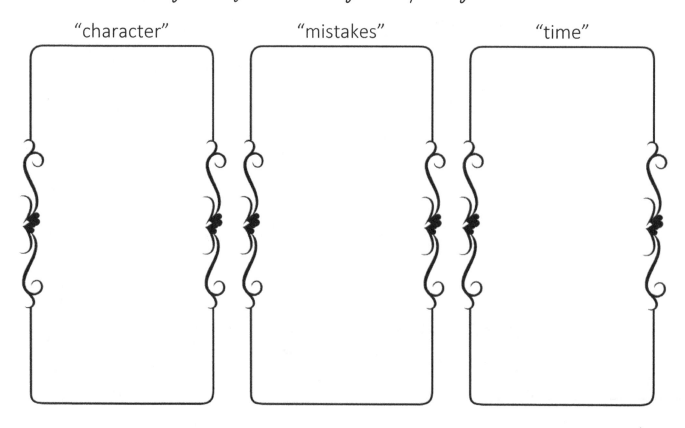

Evaluating What Californian's Say

Steve Jobs
co-founder of Apple from San Francisco

"Your work is going to fill a large part of your life, and the only way to be truly satisfied is to do what you believe is great work. And the only way to do great work is to love what you do. If you haven't found it yet, keep looking. Don't settle. As with all matters of the heart, you'll know it when you find it."

What do you love, love, love to do?

Advertisements

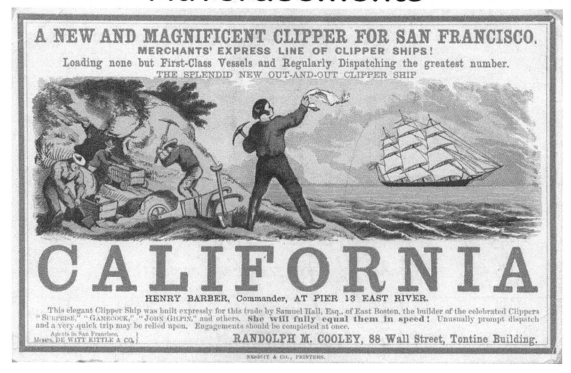

How did transportation companies make money during the Gold Rush?

ONLINE SOURCES OF INFORMATION:

The California Flag

Search for facts about the California flag: the bear, the star, and the words "California" and "Republic". Why are they there and what do they signify?

1

2

3

4

The State

Search the history of the state of California. Record three interesting or weird facts that you uncovered in your research.

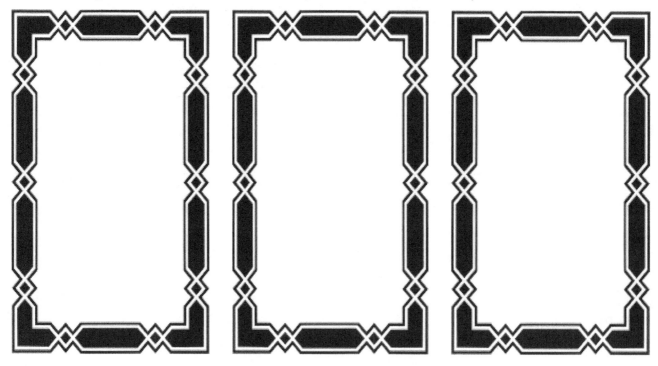

ONLINE SOURCES OF INFORMATION:

_____

_____

California Landscape

Search online for information about the landscape of California and how it made traveling <u>easy</u> or <u>difficult</u> for the "forty-niners". Write about the mountains, the rivers, the deserts, the coasts, and what people had to do in order to get from there to here.

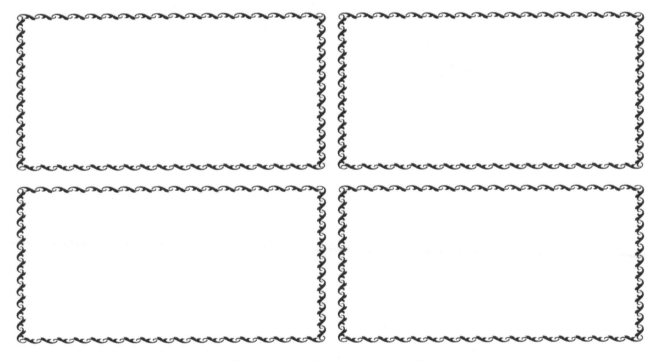

ONLINE SOURCES OF INFORMATION:

_____

_____

California Missions

By the time of the Gold Rush, how many towns had missions or churches? Why did new towns build a church as the population increased? Why were churches important to these adventurers?

1

2

3

4

ONLINE SOURCES OF INFORMATION:

_____

_____

California Forest Fires

How do forest fires start in the forest? How would early <u>pioneers</u> and <u>adventurers</u> escape the **flames** and **smoke** from a raging fire? Did humans accidentally start some of these fires? How?

ONLINE SOURCES OF INFORMATION:

How do we use gold today?

List ten things that are made of gold:

1.

2.

3.

4.

5.

6.

7.

8.

9.

10.

ONLINE SOURCES OF INFORMATION:

_____

_____

Boomtowns

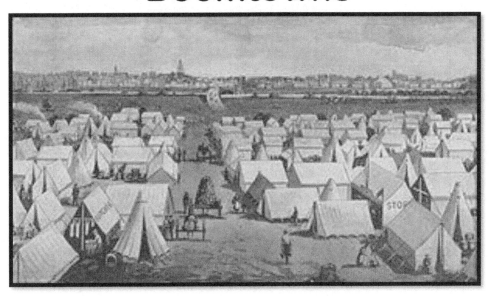

What do you notice about this boomtown scene?

1.

2.

3.

4.

5.

6.

7.

The Shoshone Tribe

What is special about this indigenous tribe of California? Go online and search for information about their <u>history</u> and <u>people</u>, their <u>religion</u> and where they <u>lived</u>, their <u>leaders</u> and the <u>language</u> they spoke.

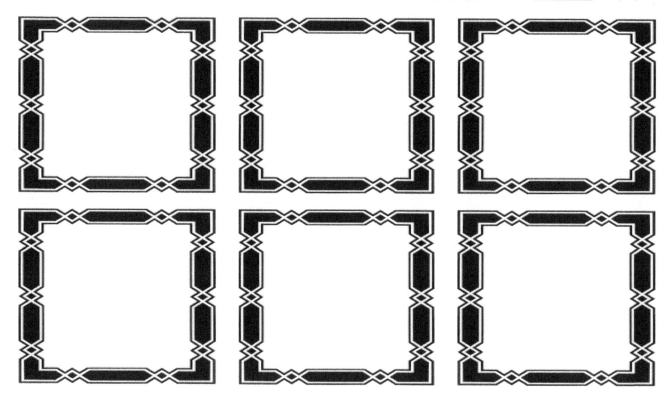

ONLINE SOURCES OF INFORMATION:

_____

_____

The Timbisha Tribe

What is special about this indigenous tribe of California? Go online and search for information about their <u>history</u> and <u>people</u>, their <u>religion</u> and where they <u>lived</u>, their <u>leaders</u> and the <u>language</u> they spoke.

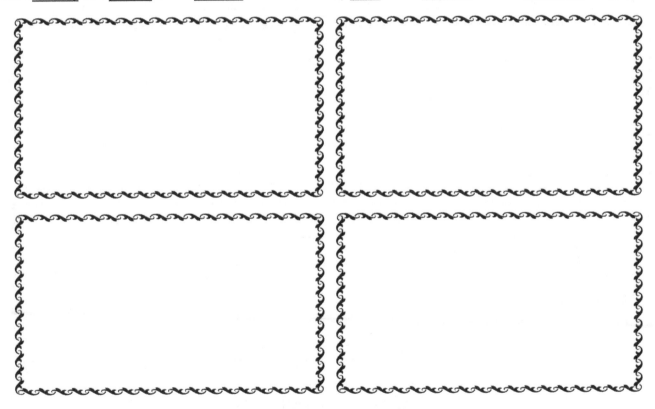

ONLINE SOURCES OF INFORMATION:

_____

_____

The Tolowa Tribe

What is special about this indigenous tribe of California? Go online and search for information about their <u>history</u> and <u>people</u>, their <u>religion</u> and where they <u>lived</u>, their <u>leaders</u> and the <u>language</u> they spoke.

ONLINE SOURCES OF INFORMATION:

The Tongva Tribe

What is special about this indigenous tribe of California? Go online and search for information about their <u>history</u> and <u>people</u>, their <u>religion</u> and where they <u>lived</u>, their <u>leaders</u> and the <u>language</u> they spoke.

ONLINE SOURCES OF INFORMATION:

The Wappo Tribe

What is special about this indigenous tribe of California? Go online and search for information about their <u>history</u> and <u>people</u>, their <u>religion</u> and where they <u>lived</u>, their <u>leaders</u> and the <u>language</u> they spoke.

 ❶

 ❷

 ❸

 ❹

ONLINE SOURCES OF INFORMATION:

1)	2)	3)

The Washoe Tribe

What is special about this indigenous tribe of California? Go online and search for information about their <u>history</u> and <u>people</u>, their <u>religion</u> and where they <u>lived</u>, their <u>leaders</u> and the <u>language</u> they spoke.

ONLINE SOURCES OF INFORMATION:

The Wintu Tribe

What is special about this indigenous tribe of California? Go online and search for information about their <u>history</u> and <u>people</u>, their <u>religion</u> and where they <u>lived</u>, their <u>leaders</u> and the <u>language</u> they spoke.

1

2

3

4

ONLINE SOURCES OF INFORMATION: :

The Yana Tribe

What is special about this indigenous tribe of California? Go online and search for information about their <u>history</u> and <u>people</u>, their <u>religion</u> and where they <u>lived</u>, their <u>leaders</u> and the <u>language</u> they spoke.

ONLINE SOURCES OF INFORMATION:

_____

_____

The Yokuts Tribe

What is special about this indigenous tribe of California? Go online and search for information about their <u>history</u> and <u>people</u>, their <u>religion</u> and where they <u>lived</u>, their <u>leaders</u> and the <u>language</u> they spoke.

ONLINE SOURCES OF INFORMATION:

The Yuki Tribe

What is special about this indigenous tribe of California? Go online and search for information about their <u>history</u> and <u>people</u>, their <u>religion</u> and where they <u>lived</u>, their <u>leaders</u> and the <u>language</u> they spoke.

1

2

3

4

ONLINE SOURCES OF INFORMATION:

The Yurok Tribe

What is special about this indigenous tribe of California? Go online and search for information about their <u>history</u> and <u>people</u>, their <u>religion</u> and where they <u>lived</u>, their <u>leaders</u> and the <u>language</u> they spoke.

_____
_____
_____
_____
_____
_____
_____
_____
_____
_____
_____
_____

ONLINE SOURCES OF INFORMATION:

⬇

_____
_____

The Indigenous Peoples of America

1.

2.

3.

4.

5.

6.

7.

8.

9.

10.

ONLINE SOURCES OF INFORMATION:

1)	2)	3)

Indigenous People: Visited by Strangers

1.

2.

3.

4.

5.

6.

7.

8.

9.

10.

ONLINE SOURCES OF INFORMATION:

1)	2)	3)

Indigenous People: Surviving Off the Land

1.

2.

3.

4.

5.

6.

7.

8.

9.

10.

ONLINE SOURCES OF INFORMATION:

1)	2)	3)

Indigenous Peoples
of
California

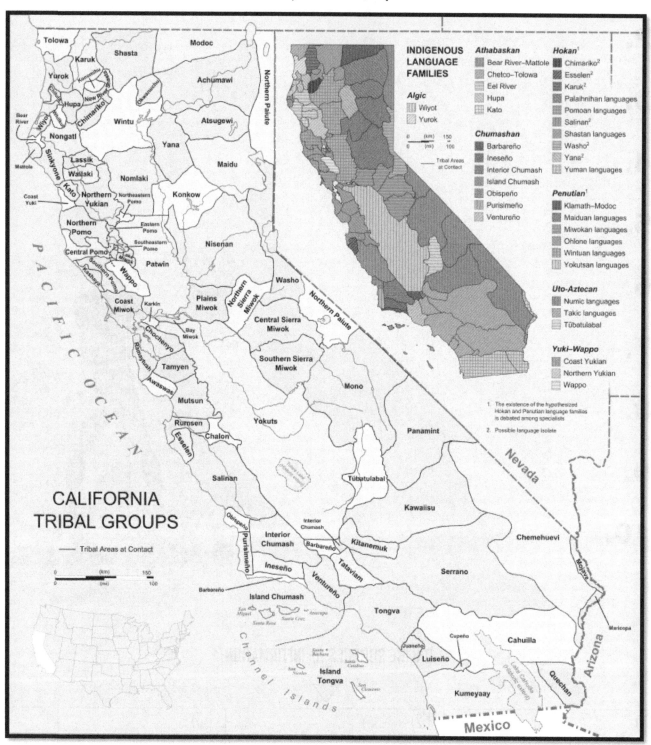

https://en.wikipedia.org/wiki/Indigenous_peoples_of_California

Point Reyes National Seashore

What is special about this popular California tourist destination? Why has the US Government set aside this land so that people can visit here and explore? Research online and share what you learn:

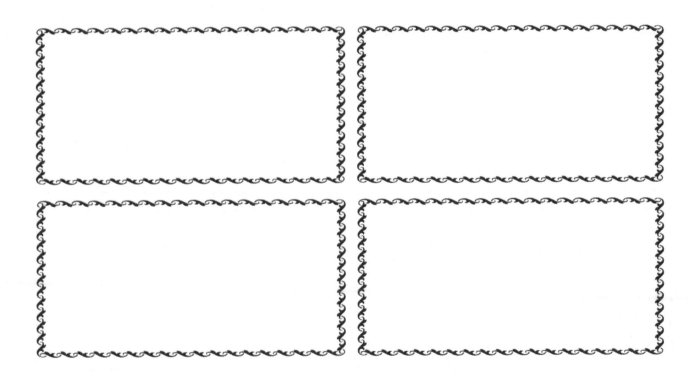

ONLINE SOURCES OF INFORMATION:

_____

_____

Port Chicago Naval Magazine
National Monument

What is special about this popular California tourist destination? Why has the US Government set aside this land so that people can visit here and explore? Research online and share what you learn:

ONLINE SOURCES OF INFORMATION:

Presidio of San Francisco

What is special about this popular California tourist destination? Why has the US Government set aside this land so that people can visit here and explore? Research online and share what you learn:

ONLINE SOURCES OF INFORMATION:

Redwood National Park

What is special about this popular California tourist destination? Why has the US Government set aside this land so that people can visit here and explore? Research online and share what you learn:

ONLINE SOURCES OF INFORMATION:

_____

_____

Rosie the Riveter WWII Home Front National Historic Park

What is special about this popular California tourist destination? Why has the US Government set aside this land so that people can visit here and explore? Research online and share what you learn:

ONLINE SOURCES OF INFORMATION:

San Francisco Maritime National Historical Park

What is special about this popular California tourist destination? Why has the US Government set aside this land so that people can visit here and explore? Research online and share what you learn:

1

2

3

4

ONLINE SOURCES OF INFORMATION: :

_____

_____

Santa Monica Mountains National Recreation Area

What is special about this popular California tourist destination? Why has the US Government set aside this land so that people can visit here and explore? Research online and share what you learn:

1

2

3

ONLINE SOURCES OF INFORMATION:

Sequoia National Park

What is special about this popular California tourist destination? Why has the US Government set aside this land so that people can visit here and explore? Research online and share what you learn:

ONLINE SOURCES OF INFORMATION:

Kings Canyon National Park

What is special about this popular California tourist destination? Why has the US Government set aside this land so that people can visit here and explore? Research online and share what you learn:

1

2

3

4

ONLINE SOURCES OF INFORMATION:

Tule Lake Unit

What is special about this popular California tourist destination? Why has the US Government set aside this land so that people can visit here and explore? Research online and share what you learn:

_____

_____

_____

_____

_____

_____

_____

_____

_____

_____

_____

_____

ONLINE SOURCES OF INFORMATION:

⬇

_____

_____

Whiskeytown National Recreation Area

What is special about this popular California tourist destination? Why has the US Government set aside this land so that people can visit here and explore? Research online and share what you learn:

ONLINE SOURCES OF INFORMATION:

_____

_____

Yosemite National Park

What is special about this popular California tourist destination? Why has the US Government set aside this land so that people can visit here and explore? Research online and share what you learn:

1

2

3

4

ONLINE SOURCES OF INFORMATION:

_____

_____

National Parks

List ten activities or actions that require money:

1.

2.

3.

4.

5.

6.

7.

8.

9.

10.

ONLINE SOURCES OF INFORMATION:

_____

_____

Protecting the Land

List ten things that are made of gold:

1.

2.

3.

4.

5.

6.

7.

8.

9.

10.

ONLINE SOURCES OF INFORMATION:

_____

_____

Yosemite National Park

What do you notice about these two stamps honoring Yosemite National Park

1.

2.

3.

4.

5.

California Politics: Jerry Brown

Use a laptop, tablet or phone to access the internet and explore this California politician.

Age:

Gender:

Place of birth:

Ethnicity:

Political affiliation:

Job title:

Search for four interesting facts that you learned about them in your research:

1

2

3

4

SOURCES:

_____

_____

California Politics: Nancy Pelosi

Use a laptop, tablet or phone to access the internet and explore this California politician.

Age:
Gender:
Place of birth:
Ethnicity:
Political affiliation:
Job title:

Search for three interesting facts that you learned about them in your research:

SOURCES:

_____

_____

California Politics: Diane Feinstein

Use a laptop, tablet or phone to access the internet and explore this California politician.

Age:

Gender:

Place of birth:

Ethnicity:

Political affiliation:

Job title:

Search for four interesting facts that you learned about them in your research:

SOURCES:

_____

_____

California Politics: Kamala Harris

Use a laptop, tablet or phone to access the internet and explore this California politician.

Age:

Gender:

Place of birth:

Ethnicity:

Political affiliation:

Job title:

Search for interesting facts that you learned about them in your research:

_____

_____

_____

_____

_____

_____

_____

_____

_____

SOURCES:

_____

_____

California Politics: Adam Schiff

Use a laptop, tablet or phone to access the internet and explore this California politician.

Age:

Gender:

Place of birth:

Ethnicity:

Political affiliation:

Job title:

Search for four interesting facts that you learned about them in your research:

1 _____

2 _____

3 _____

4 _____

SOURCES:

_____

_____

California Politics: Grace Napolitano

Use a laptop, tablet or phone to access the internet and explore this California politician.

Age:

Gender:

Place of birth:

Ethnicity:

Political affiliation:

Job title:

Search for four interesting facts that you learned about them in your research:

SOURCES:

California Politics: Devin Nunes

Use a laptop, tablet or phone to access the internet and explore this California politician.

Age:

Gender:

Place of birth:

Ethnicity:

Political affiliation:

Job title:

Search for four interesting facts that you learned about them in your research:

 ➊

 ➋

 ➌

 ➍

SOURCES:

_____

_____

What is the job of a politician?

List ten activities or actions that a politician is responsible for:

1.

2.

3.

4.

5.

6.

7.

8.

9.

10.

SOURCES:

_____

_____

What is the job of a US Senator?

List ten activities or actions that a US Senator is responsible for:

1.

2.

3.

4.

5.

6.

7.

8.

9.

10.

SOURCES:

_____

_____

What is the job of a US Representative?

List ten activities or actions that a US Representative is responsible for:

1.

2.

3.

4.

5.

6.

7.

8.

9.

10.

SOURCES:

_____

_____

What is the job of a Governor?

List ten activities or actions that a Governor is responsible for:

1.

2.

3.

4.

5.

6.

7.

8.

9.

10.

SOURCES:

_____

_____

Sacramento, California

Use a <u>laptop</u>, <u>tablet</u> or <u>phone</u> to access the internet and explore the city of **Sacramento**. Record five interesting facts you discovered about this California city below.

1

2

3

4

5

SOURCES:

Oakland, California

OAKLAND

Use a <u>laptop</u>, <u>tablet</u> or <u>phone</u> to access the internet and explore the city of **Oakland**. Record five interesting facts you discovered about this California city below.

1

2

3

4

5

SOURCES:

Catalina Island, California

Use a <u>laptop</u>, <u>tablet</u> or <u>phone</u> to access the internet and explore the city of **Catalina Island**. Record five interesting facts you discovered about this California city below.

SOURCES:

Anaheim, California

Use a laptop, tablet or phone to access the internet and explore the city of **Anaheim**. Record five interesting facts you discovered about this California city below.

1

2

3

4

5

SOURCES:

Palm Springs, California

Use a <u>laptop</u>, <u>tablet</u> or <u>phone</u> to access the internet and explore the city of **Palm Springs**. Record several interesting facts you discovered about this California city below.

_____

_____

_____

_____

_____

_____

_____

_____

_____

_____

_____

_____

_____

_____

_____

_____

SOURCES:

_____

_____

Riverside, California

Use a <u>laptop</u>, <u>tablet</u> or <u>phone</u> to access the internet and explore the city of **Riverside**. Record five interesting facts you discovered about this California city below.

1

2

3

4

5

SOURCES:

Big Bear, California

Use a <u>laptop</u>, <u>tablet</u> or <u>phone</u> to access the internet and explore the city of **Big Bear**. Record several interesting facts you discovered about this California city below.

_____

_____

_____

_____

_____

_____

_____

_____

_____

_____

_____

_____

_____

_____

_____

_____

_____

_____

SOURCES:

_____

_____

Beverly Hills, California

Use a <u>laptop</u>, <u>tablet</u> or <u>phone</u> to access the internet and explore the city of **Beverly Hills**. Record seven interesting facts you discovered about this California city below.

1

2

3

4

5

6

7

SOURCES:

_____

_____

Hollywood, California

Use a <u>laptop</u>, <u>tablet</u> or <u>phone</u> to access the internet and explore the city of **Hollywood**. Record three interesting facts you discovered about this California city below.

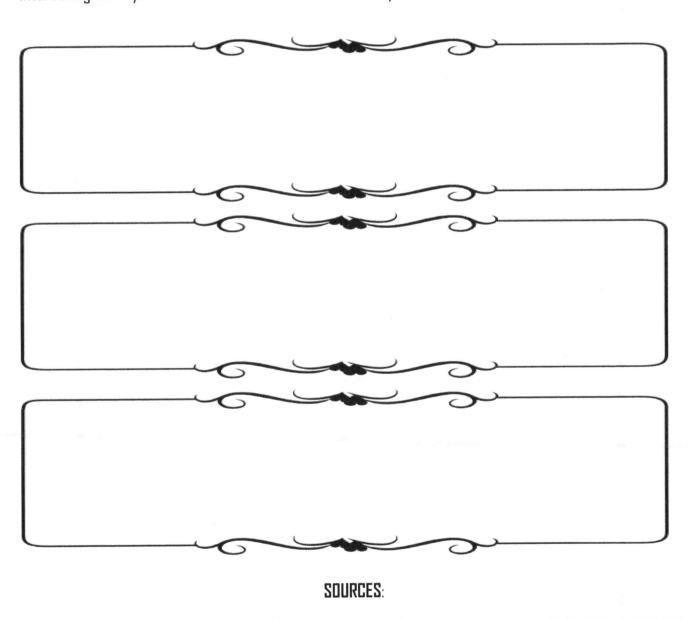

SOURCES:

_____

_____

California State Flag

California State Quarter

California State Seal

California State Map

Made in United States
Orlando, FL
22 August 2022

21375219R00070